COATLICUE GIRL

A Bilingual Collection of Poems and Stories

GRIS MUÑOZ

Foreword by Luis Alberto Urrea

flowersong
BOOKS

FlowerSong Books
McAllen, Texas 78501

Copyright © 2019 by Gris Muñoz

ISBN: 978-1-7338092-4-5

Published by FlowerSong Books
in the United States of America.
www.flowersongbooks.com

Set in Adobe Garamond Pro

Cover art and illustrations by Los Dos
Photograph by Carlos Gutiérrez
Typeset by Matthew Revert

No part of this book may be reproduced without written permission from the publisher.

All inquiries and permission requests should be addressed to the Publisher.

COATLICUE · GIRL

Poems and Stories

GRIS MUÑOZ

Foreword
Luis Alberto Urrea

Tonantzin in El Paso

I first became aware of Gris during my many visits to El Paso related first to my books about The Saint of Cabora. My tia, Teresita. I hung out with the Byrds, of Cinco Punto Press, and my friend Benjamin Saenz. Crawled cemeteries and Segundo Barrio. Shopped for curandera herbs in Juarez. Then came back to write about the town for various publications.

At the height of the narco depredations across the river, Gris appeared in my inbox.

Having come up amidst the Chicano revolutionary days, a time when we were all seemingly a familia, we all worked on mad projects and world-saving Quixotadas, and nobody was ever formal with each other, I fell right in with her. Esta Gris seemed to believe, like I still do, that it is 1977 and we are all together saving the Raza and the country. She reminded me of all the homies and warriors I knew then

--Alurista, Angela de Hoyos, Ricardo Sanchez, Lorna Dee Cervantes, Rudy Anaya. You can fill in the blanks: pick any santa or santo who stood up and cried out for us.

Although she was discreet about her output, I slowly became aware of her writing, and of her dreams. And I was thrilled when the many words she was crafting and sharing in anthologies and journals coalesced into this first book. It is a vivid, wind-swept thing, this ritual. Multi-lingual, woven with faiths that are ancient and various and somehow one. Feminist, ancient, sophisticated and fervent. Gris moves from poetry to prose and back again. Like so many great Chicana scriptures laid down in our pasts, this is an announcement of arrival and a crie de coeur.

But let us never forget it is also a crie de guerre.

This is the border, cabrones, the mero desierto. This is Apache blood in the veins. This is a dancer and a poet and a healer talking. A rock and roll curandera with a syncretistic religious heart. Tossing off chains as she goes.

I soon started to recognize Gris. I started to see the same spirit that moved in Teresita, La Santa. And the medicine women who taught me their secrets so I could write my books. That's when I started calling her Tonantzin.

So happy this immense journey has begun. May many travel with you, hermanita.

                        L.A.U.
                        Chicago c/s

Acknowledgements

This collection is dedicated to my daughter, Belen Xochicoatl, and my parents, Antonio and Concepcion Muñoz - my raíces in this realm. Gracias, Creador, for their lives. Los amo!

Luis Alberto Urrea, my mentor and friend: Your joy is medicine. I give thanks for your life and role in this world. Thank you for your unending humor, support, acceptance and strength, Jefeaux. Thank you for still taking the time to be curious.

I have had the honor of having had my spirit healed by several spiritual Abuelas and Abuelos. Abuela Beatriz Villegas, Abuela Cristal Gonzalez, Abuela Rosa Tupina Yaotonalcuauhtli, Rocio Cihualcoatl de Chiapas, Abuelo Pete Duarte, Abuelo Carlos Aceves. Abuelo Ramon Arroyos on the other side. Jesus Castañeda que me salvó la vida. I remember you all constantly. Tlazocamati a todxs por sus enseñanzas, sus momentos de poder, de perdon, de amor. Sus cantos.

Cemelli De Aztlan, ceremonial sister and dear friend: Thank you for lending me your liver. I love you.

Felicia Montes, I don't know if I would be here without you. Eres mi hermana de ombligo. Thank you for always being the example Fe, you humble me and always teach with love. Thank you for bringing Maria Rivera into my life.

Terese Mailhot, you push me and that's something. You've always kept our goals in sight. You always believed we'd be read one day, that we'd have words, words that matter. I love you, Sis. Watching you thrive is inspiring and real.

K-Sue Park, sometimes kin appears when you least expect. I feel stronger when you're around.
My city misses you.

Rachel Cheek, thank you for all of your love, support and tenderness. Te adoro, magic one. Looking forward to seeing your voice fly in this world!

For Melissa Flores, wherever you are.

Mi Corazon and better half, Marky Silva. Mi keeper of fires. I love you, amor.

This collection is honored to be accompanied by original artwork from Lxs Dos, Christian and Ramon Cardenas. Thank you for your humor, talent and care. You made it magic.

To Edward and Liliana Vidaurre, Thank you for your vision and unending kindness.

For all the wandering ones, you are yet to bloom.

Creator, you are walking with me. Thank you for my life.

have you
never heard the fire singing singing as if every sound hurt as if every note was pulled from deep within and the leap from emotion to sound left a wound
                              ragged and bleeding but give me that song it is the song i need to stay true the fire has come the fire has sung

                                        ire'ne lara silva

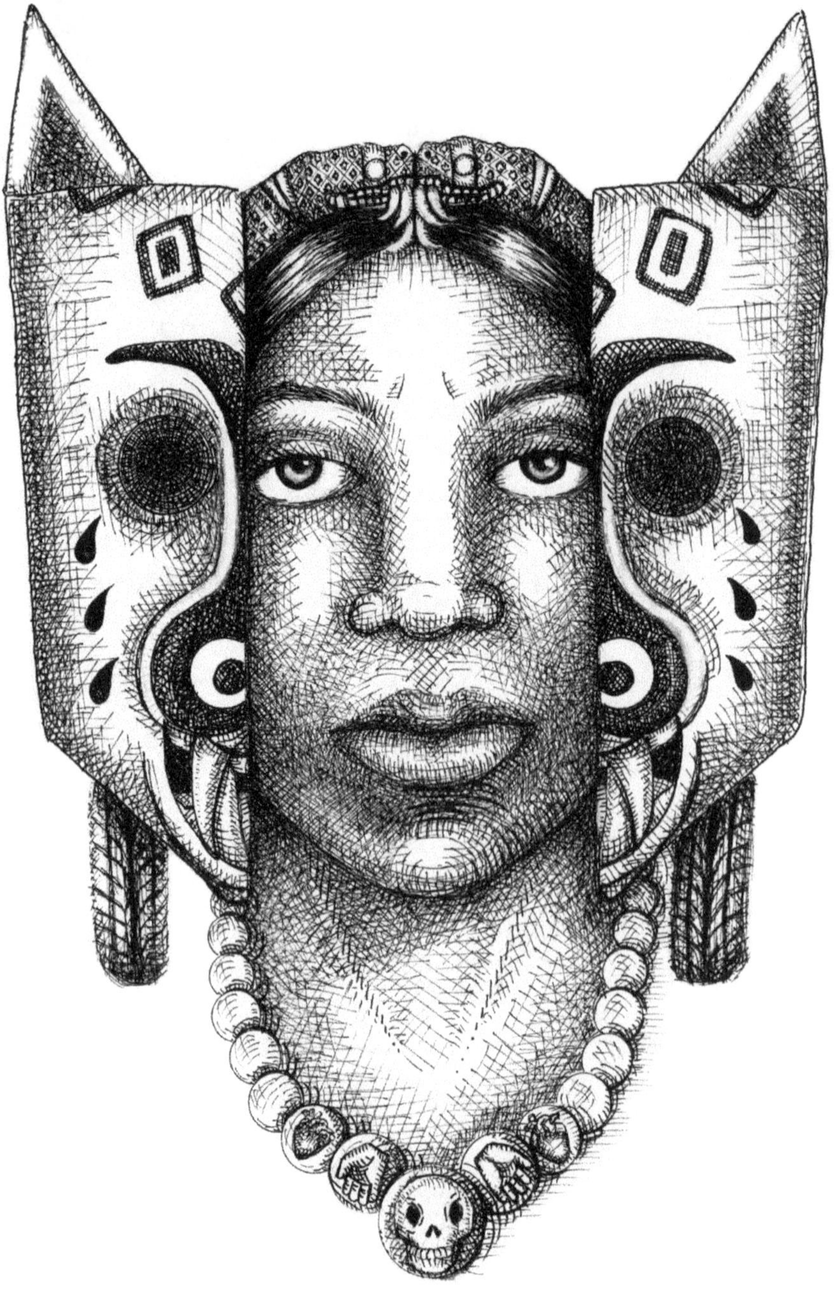

Sometimes

Sometimes
I
do
not
want
to
remember
their
eyes
my
folded
fangs
to
them
and
how
alone
I
felt
snake
under
the
skirts

El Maíz

Nací dentro de un carro Chevrolet
magueyes en maceta en el U.S. of A.
Mi tierra sagrada ni conoce mi cara
Y el maíz se ha hecho cornflais.

Mi tierra sagrada ni conoce mi cara,
y
el
maíz
se
ha
hecho
cornflais.

Fronteriza

Oye mi canto de peregrina,
tierra floreada, tierra querida
soy una de tus hijas fronterizas
y te quiero confesar:
que he despreciado y he maltratado
a mi Mexicanidad.

De mi otro yo,
mi otro lado
yo me había olvidado.

Cuando era chiquilla
aprendí ingles fácil
y yo me reía
de las muchachitas
que no podían.

Después me enamore con la cultura norteamericana
hasta tuve ganas de cambiar mi cara
mi nariz Maya
fue regalada a doctores que me cortaron con calma
después de promesas de plata.

Linda tierra de mi abuela patria,
no me des la espalda
que

aunque ahora lloro dentro de mi falda larga,
es cierto que por años solo te visitaba
para andar por tus calles
enviciada y tomada.

Cantinas y noches largas
entre sueños de narcos y cuentos de hadas
con la muerte yo jugaba
bailando en tacones de plata
y en la banqueta quebrada
caminaba
como princesa
entre tu pobreza
y mis hermanas gastadas.

Beer Run

Wrought iron swirls adorned the windows and there was a hastily built fence outside the small rectangular house where I grew up. Up until the time I was a teenager, the whole yard had been completely covered in grass, but once my older brothers moved out my dad decided he didn't want to keep up the lawn anymore. I stayed the longest of us four, like I was supposed to, but was never expected to do any yard work. Soon after my last brother left, a cement truck rolled up the driveway and pumped smooth grey sludge over it all, making the house look like it was surrounded by an empty parking lot.

Years later, when it was sweltering hot, I especially liked sitting outside on the hood of my faded grey Cavalier after my parents had gone to bed and rolling a joint, smoking and watching all of the late-night cars parking at the convenience store across the street. I'd wonder who was inside, and where they were going.

When I was six, I wrote a letter to McGruff the Crime Dog, a cartoon bloodhound I'd see on television. McGruff was first introduced in the eighties to combat societal drug use. Similar to Smokey the Bear, McGruff was staunchly against illegal activities and substances. In the handmade construction paper card I'd sent him, I also made a solemn pledge to never do any drugs. Six weeks later I received a package in the mail filled to the brim with McGruff paraphernalia: stickers, masks, and even a small badge I wore proudly, vowing to keep the neighborhood safe.

I wondered what McGruff would think of me now.

"Sorry, fucker. I guess I disappointed you, too," I said aloud, as I pulled out a small sandwich bag filled with what Redbeard had called 'Lima-Limon'. The buds were pretty, a bright, almost technicolor green. Their scent would waft under your nose when you opened the bag, citrusy and light.
I've always liked rolling joints. I've found it's a good skill to have, even if you don't smoke.

First, you have to have something to break it up on. If it's a piece of paper, fold it in half length-wise to avoid any falling shake. Hold the bud between your thumb and forefinger and with your other hand, break a few bits off. Next the rubbing, rubbing into those bits until they dismantle, and then you pull all of the stems and seeds off and out. Fold the rolling paper almost in half, making sure the crease is sharp, and lick the edge of it slowly so you can tear a little piece off. I learned that from someone somewhere along the way, it's so you don't get as much paper in your smoke.

With the folded rolling paper sitting in your left hand, reach over with your right and take a small pinch out of the little broken up pile, and line it smoothly along the crease. When you're done, grasp onto each side. The tricky part is keeping it straight, holding the tiny paper on each side with both hands so it can be rolled. I'll smooth it, pressing it closer and tighter together, and then carefully twist each edge until the ends are perfectly shut. The really good rollers know how to make the side you light different than the edge you put between your lips. I'm not sure why I never picked up that skill.

When we first started getting high, I liked the papers that had cherries or peaches printed on them, but now I don't mind the little ones that come with packs of rolling tobacco. I like to roll them long and thin, tight, with the joint hanging out of my mouth I'll light the fire, whatever fire.

A softly revving Camaro pulled into my sight. It was ruddy-hued, a light brown or maybe tan. I watched blankly as it parked across the street, tires lined up against the fading curb. It took me a moment to figure out what was going on and then I took a deep hit and held it, watching with interest.

Beer run. I've been witnessing beer runs since I was a little girl. As soon as my mother would see a car creeping up that curb with the lights off, she'd frantically call me inside and quickly lock the door. I'd run and turn off all of the lights in the house. "Para que no nos vean," she'd say.
We'd sit cowering inside, huddled close together until we heard it, sometimes shouts or breaking glass and then always the sound of a car door smashing shut, an engine booming and tires squealing away. I remember once hearing gunshots, the taste of my dry mouth hanging in fear. We were afraid, always afraid. Of the men who stole beer and held up stores with little

black guns and folded bandanas covering their menacing faces.

Criminals. Criminales. Bestias. Beasts.

Redbeard broke it down once when we were blazing.

"Punks," he declared. "Only chapetillos steal beer like that, desperate high schoolers and shit. Ain't no real motherfuckin' criminal going to risk getting chased down by some dumbass good samaritan, or the cops for something as stupid as a thirty pack. The real motherfuckers think before they act, I assure you," he declared diplomatically, and then taking a hit, breathed out and spoke at the same time.

"The real criminals buy their beer before midnight."

Post-beer run is another story. The cops show up and sometimes shut down the store depending on how severe the situation got.

This one was in progress. I watched the Camaro exhibit the telltale combo of running engine and lights off. Laughing a little, I thought of Redbeard. Just by the looks of the car, I knew he was right. Something about it, a feeling I got.

"Hijole," I whispered, taking a hit. "Either these fools want to get caught, or they just don't give a fuck."

It was time to investigate. I was thirsty, anyway. I slid off the hood and lightly dabbed some saliva on my finger to put out the joint, and then carefully placed it on one of the windshield wipers before walking across the street toward the sitting car.

The driver's side window was open and without much hesitation I stuck my head into the vehicle, peering inside. There were five teenage boys in there, all wearing some variation of Polo top and khaki short. Redbeard had been right all along. The driver had a scrawny-haired chin and half-ass mustache, and he leaned back and stretched in his seat like he was afraid.

"You guys going to do a beer run?"

No one responded and instead they all began meeting each other's darting eyes. It was obvious not one of them owned the car. The driver looked about seventeen and had probably borrowed it from his pops or big brother. Damn shame, if only he knew where his baby was.

"Look, I know you are, and I don't care what you guys do. I live in this hood though, and I was on my way to the 7-11 for an orange soda. Can you wait until I do that, because if you jack the beer, they might shut down the store and call the cops, and I smell like herb, 'cause I've been blazing it."

No one spoke, and instead they all rested their gaze on the driver, who after a moment of hesitation met my eyes and responded. "Okay, but don't fuck us over."

We had an agreement.

They weren't even stoners, I could tell.

Yeah, I was fucking with them. Maybe I was bored. I backed away from the car and headed in the direction of the store. Once inside, I went toward the back and grabbed my soda from the cooler, all the while sizing up the new evening clerk, a brown-haired girl with droopy eyes framed with shaggy bangs. A nametag spelling out 'Anabel' hung silently off the store's mandatory orange smock.

I wondered if this was her first beer run and how she'd react.

"You'll be alright, Anabel," I whispered to myself silently as I paid. "Those guys were dumbasses for sure."

I felt their relief when I walked out of the store and passed in front of their car with my soda and a last-minute decision Hershey Bar. It was dark but I could see that the guy sitting in the back right of the car walked out and slowly made a beeline towards the store.

I relit my joint and waited, puffing excitedly. A couple of minutes later there was a loud smash, and then I saw him running for the car, a 30-pack in each hand. The Camaro then revving and booming and the door swinging open as he threw the beer and jumped in behind it. The car then took off all bat out of hell and shit, as eager as they were.

I couldn't believe they had actually waited for me to buy my soda.

"Dumbfucks," I laughed.

Costco

My mom loves Costco now, she used to love Sam's Club. Her eyes widen and get giddy once she's there.

"Griselda, búscame un carrito."

I'll lose her at some point after spending a few seconds too long sorting through a pile of oversized coffee tins, and then eventually find her two aisles over carrying a sack of elbow macaroni under one arm and a bucket of Tide under the other.

This visit wasn't any different. We waded through the sample area, where the crowd of shoppers had thickened. It was because a skinny, blonde spiky-haired employee was about to begin a knife presentation. He looked about nineteen or twenty and kept checking his watch nervously. I watched him adjust his belt a couple of times and eventually step up onto a little platform surrounded by rows of tuna cans and pickles. He tried to muster up enough energy to look enthusiastic.

"Quédate aquí, voy a buscar spinach. No te muevas, a veces regalan cuchillos."

"Okay, mom."

I stood next to a Señora holding a rotisserie chicken and together we watched the kid set up his knife kit. "Tiene buenos cuchillos," she whispered. "Si," I whispered back. It was a whole thing now, the area around the kid had been taken up, we all looked up and waited.

My grandfather had been the butcher in Guadalupe Bravo, Chihuahua, a tiny speck of town somewhere on the border not too far from Juarez.

Many times, I've thought I had it in me to be a butcher, too.

The kid was a couple of minutes into his presentation now, so far, no giveaways. He'd gone through the paring, peeling and boning knives impressively; chopping potatoes, julienning carrots, then slicing bone, cardboard, aluminum. It wasn't boring. Some people walked away but the Señora and I stayed on, along with several others.

By now there was a new Señor in our group, he was wearing a blue T-shirt and a cap that read 'Bimbo' across the front. He was holding a paper cocktail plate with a few buffalo wings on it.

Next up was a half-inch steel bar. The guy showed the crowd the serrated utility knife and began sawing away. It was working, and after a few seconds, he stopped and presented the indentation the knife had made on the steel. He asked if there were any buyers and everyone stayed silent, watching him, hoping he'd up the ante.

Suddenly Bimbo cap said, "Mejor que los vaya a vender en Juárez, a los carteles." The crowd tittered. "Si, verdad," responded another voice from behind me, "Así cortan pescuezos rapidin." We all laughed, si, verdad, si, mejor en Juárez, pescuezos, rapidin. Someone said he should sell them door to door over there. I don't know why but, in that moment, we laughed even harder.

We lost it when he pulled out the butcher knife. I saw the Señora pull a little crushed up Kleenex out of her pocket and dab the corners of her eyes, her face distorted. The blond kid looked up at everyone, looked confused for a moment and then giggled, assuming we were just really enjoying his presentation.

Manflowers

There was a house on the other side of our block. "Allí viven las manfloras," my mom would say, the disgust in her voice palpable. "Si algún día te ofrecen comida, no la tomes." Whenever we had to walk by she would grasp onto my hand even tighter and hurry me along. The house didn't really look any different from others on the block. It was white brick with a forest green trim and there was a grey pebble walkway down the middle of the yard that led to the door.

There was always so much noise and movement at our house. I liked riding my bike out of there, pedaling down our driveway and taking the sidewalk away from everyone. My mom wouldn't mind if I was gone unless I was gone too long. Once I was really going, I'd count the thin lines that separated the sidewalk into neat squares, feeling each bump under my tires.

Las Manfloras. I was pretty sure I knew what it meant. Women who were like men, who lived together like lovers. I liked the word manflowers better. I'd say it in my head and think about the word, imagining what type of plant manflowers would be if they really existed.

Following the curve of the sidewalk, I'd ride faster, picking up speed until I was close, and then I'd glide past their house. There was a gnarled wild blackberry tree in the yard and at the base of it, a growth of succulents that were always freshly watered.

Moras. The blackberries were called moras and my parents thought they were a nuisance. My dad would say they were too bitter to eat and complain how in the summer, the moras would hang fat and heavy until they stained the sidewalk because our neighbor Chuy was too lazy to look after his trees.

My friend Rosie lived on that side of the block and when I'd go over, her mom would let us ride our bikes anywhere on the street. We liked the moras. When we'd get to the manflowers' house, we'd slow down and walk our bikes up their driveway. There would be purple stains all over the sidewalk and front yard, and we'd gather the plumpest ones and pile them in our bike baskets for pretend doll food.

We'd eat them instead, laughing and squeezing as we plunged them into our mouths, the juice sanguine and bitter. Sitting crouched, I'd look up and notice Rosie's smiling face. It was spotted with moving shadows from leaves that in flashes, blocked the sunlight.

It wasn't until after I became a single mother that I learned about queer brown love, how it was the truest; like wrapping your arms around your very own skin in another body. The scent of body lotion and familiar. It was the first woman I loved who'd gently said, "I think you have post-partem depression, sweetheart." No one else had noticed. My daughter was almost two.

Ana. She'd stop by on Saturday mornings with groceries. "You didn't have to," I'd say, but she knew we were probably a little hungry. I'd boil sweet potatoes as Belen sat and tapped plastic measuring cups against the kitchen tile.

I'm on my way to see Cat Eyes. We met out dancing. I remember noticing her joy, how evident it was as she moved to the cumbias the live band was playing. Nervously, I had a couple of shots of tequila before catching her eye and holding my arm out, asking her to dance. I'd never had that feeling, of a woman's body and her moving near me, the perfume off her shoulders and my pure joy in being. I was wearing a pair of cowboy boots and even then, had never been so graceful.

Can I tell you something about Cat Eyes? I later found out she supported herself and her babies on her own, working part-time and taking on all the duties of a full-time nursing student. She only had one night, Saturday, off from her kids every two weeks. Even if she was completely spent, she made it a point to go dancing. The rest of her everydays, she was up by 5 a.m.

It's actually my birthday and I'm parked outside her apartment. She has two hours before she has to pick up her kids. I hadn't planned on doing anything for it but when I'd mentioned it to her, she insisted on making lunch. Once inside, I sat at her kitchen table and watched her make salsa. She was roasting chiles and chopping onions next to a large granite molcajete.

"I feel special," I said, our eyes meeting.

"You are, reina," she responded.

Her apartment had plants everywhere, succulents and tiny re-potted aloes arranged, lining every counter. I got up and leaned towards her, our arms wrapped around another tightly like vines, violet mouths kissing.

Coatlicue Girl

I pressed my copper mouth
against the thin of her eyelid,
delicada
blink green-veined like
folding cricket wings

In the echoing valley
you lay beside me,
breasts-
stones

I had forgotten, Coatlicue Girl
there lives the hum of mantis,
the macaw in you

Five-hundred years later
I remember

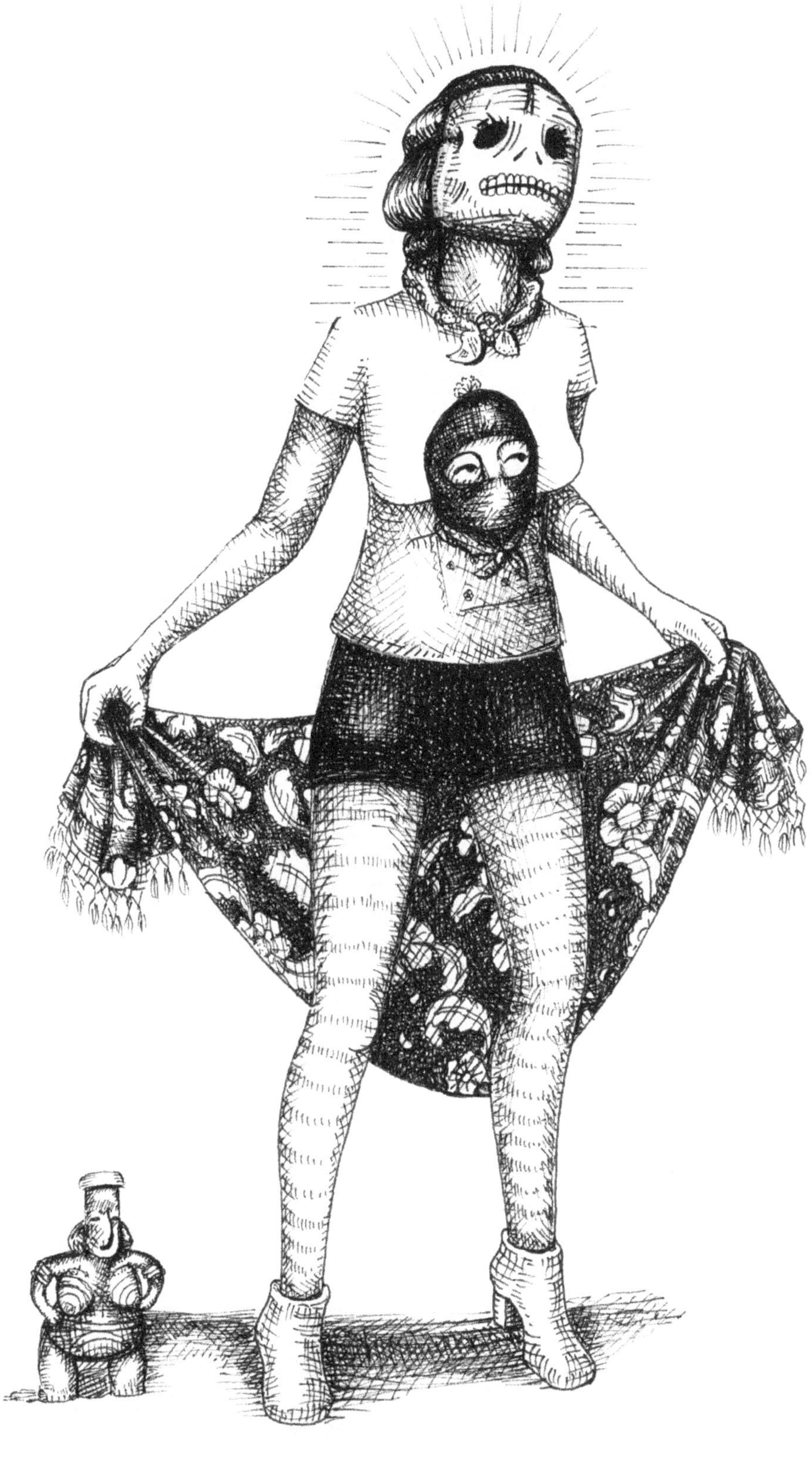

Tiny Earthquakes

In Mexico City we ran down echoing
silent grey cobblestone streets
cramped booth steamed coffee
served in white china cups
placed on blue flowered plates

Surrounded by bookshelves
we slept close to the ground
curve of your back breath loud
I wanted to reach my arm
around your waist
clumsy hands
timid restraint

Chipped white china trembling
spilled heat on flowered plates

Claudia

We never knew when it was morning,
legs entwined

I would watch her standing at the stove to make
espresso from an antique tin

A sculptor, one night she hung glass bottles from the ceiling
with twine,

they would clink with the wind

I would watch her standing at the stove to make
espresso from an antique tin

It had been her grandmother's, she said

The bottles would clink with the wind
in the basement apartment with no furniture except for
that four-poster bed

It had been her grandmother's, she had said

A sculptor, one night she hung glass bottles from the ceiling
with twine

in the basement apartment with no furniture except for

that four-poster bed

We never knew when it was morning,
legs entwined

Uncontrolled Fires

Steaming pot lids trembling
your strong legs
tender desire
pushing me up
against the counter

Calcination
shoulders and hands fast
she's drawl and swagger
ashes scatter
swirl of wind
and circumstance

Dos Pencas

Entre dos venas
dos venas
estoy,
flor de dos pencas
de dos pencas
soy.

Pajarito,
platícame de los vientos cálidos y ricos
de vivir en el cielo en tu nido escondido
que de aquí solo tomo de este río fermentado,
rendido.

Flor de agave
en la frontera vivo
y lloro
y lloro
aguardiente frío.

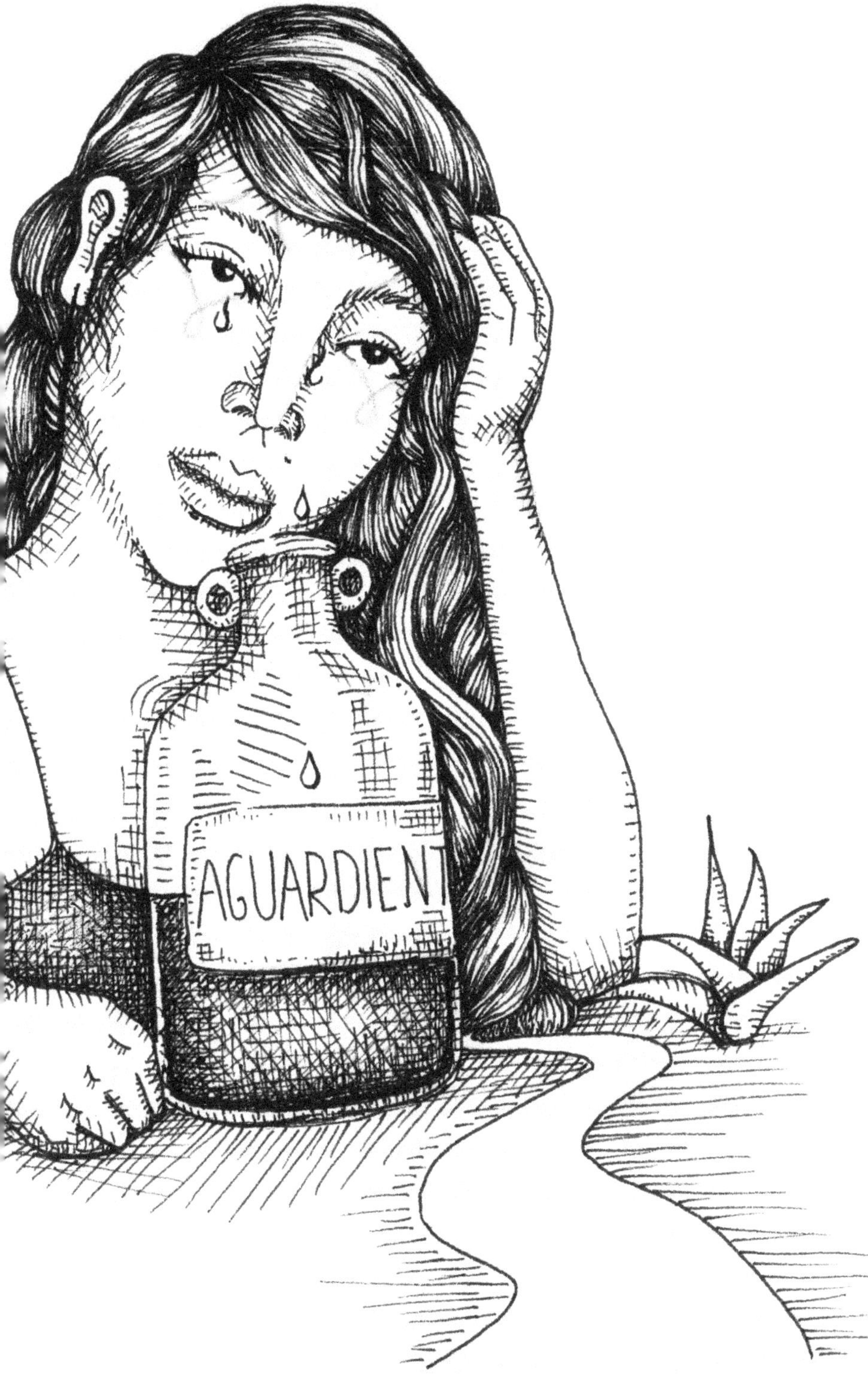
AGUARDIENT

Rivers

There
are
rivers,
crystalline
and
finely
twisted
spanning
out
like
blazing
bolts
of
lightning,
gliding
slicing
through
the
darkened
earth.

Rivers
that
end
up
bent

at
the
waist,
choked
dry
by
decisions
men
make.

Oral History

Ask me about the stories
I'd rather tell
than write.

Weekend

It was Saturday, 9:00 a.m. I'd already searched all of the purses hanging on the coatrack and any wallets stuffed into that laundry basket of clothes I kept hidden in the closet. I had found a dollar bill in the plaid backpack and another dollar smashed into the zipper compartment of a brown leather wallet my mom had given me last summer.

I smoothed out the smashed dollar and stacked them both on my bed next to a pile of change. I tried to think of any place I hadn't looked.

I'd even gone through all of my coats and jackets, even the two in the trunk of my car; quickly sticking my cupped hand into their pockets to survey for anything I'd left behind. Since I was already there, I went ahead and unlocked the door, so I could search the side and middle consoles and under the seats, only finding a fistful of dusty coins.

I went inside and added the change to the pile on the center of my bed. It looked sooty in parts and colored in others from the broken left-behind makeup in my purses. I grabbed at the pile in handfuls, dropping the coins into my kitchen colander to wash them with hand soap in the bathroom sink. Once clean, I folded the change into a towel and spread it across my bed.

I carefully began to count the change. First it was the quarters.

Every time I made a dollar with quarters, I'd put those coins into their own small stack. Then the dimes and nickels. The dimes made three piles. Three, four, five.

I had two dollar bills and five-fifty in coins. There was nothing left to pawn, so it was all I had for groceries until Monday. I'd go to the fruteria later but would have to walk to the 7-11 with my toddler as soon as she woke up from her nap. She was going to ask for milk and would not be able to wait until after the store.

I hadn't been able to breastfeed longer than a few months, but the milk hadn't really left me. I could only squeeze a few drops at a time and never much more.

When my baby woke up, I carefully dressed her, and we headed out the front door onto the sidewalk. She was almost three, and wanted to hold my hand and walk, too. The corner store was only a block from where we lived, so I figured it wouldn't be too much for her to handle.

We lived on Altura Street in Central El Paso. I'd grown up on the other side of town but eventually moved to Sunset Heights when I moved in with my daughter's father. We'd lived like artists. When we broke up, I moved to central with the baby. I would have preferred to stay in Sunset Heights, but this neighborhood was as close to the university as I could afford.

I pointed out the plants I knew the names to on the way. "Mira, these are geranios, and those are buganvilias, they're your abuela's favorites." She'd repeat the names after I said them. Right before crossing the street, I grabbed a strand of rosemary and held it to her face. "Mira mi amor, this is romero." She crinkled her nose, making me laugh. "I know, it has a strong smell, I should have warned you," I said.

We reached the store parking lot.

I noticed a luxury sports car parked somewhat near the back of the lot, near the dumpsters. I wouldn't have noticed it as much except that it was parked at an angle. It seemed out of place for this neighborhood. As we neared the store, we had to walk in front of the car, and I noticed a man sitting inside.

He was already watching me.

He was watching me in that familiar way that Mexican men do, where they hyper-focus on any body part of yours that might be used for their sexual gratification. The men around here, they don't even try to hide it. These men, these fathers and grandfathers, they eyeball indiscriminately, mentally undressing any mujeres and even any niñas over ten with a hint of tits and ass with their eyes.

I felt him watching me walking with my baby and felt a tepid anger rising in my stomach. I used to ignore them but at some point stopped being able to.

The half-gallon of milk was $2.49. I still had five dollars to buy food for the weekend. I was sad.

When we walked out the car was still there, except the man had gotten out and was leaning against the driver's side door. He looked wealthy, even in casual weekend clothes. He was tall and somewhat lean, like maybe he ran or went to the gym a couple of times a week. He was Latino, his face light-skinned with faded pockmarks on both cheeks. He was still watching me. It felt like he was waiting for me now.

He was smiling at us as we got closer.

"Hola," he said. I eyed him and kept walking. He tried again, this time in English. "Hi, excuse me, do you speak English?"

I stopped, and as much as I didn't want to, said, "Yes." I figured he needed directions somewhere.

"Hi. I'm uh, I'm actually looking for a young woman to clean my house a few times a week. I live over by the mountain and pay very well." He focused on my chest. "Do you happen to know any young mothers or students that could use some extra money? Would you be interested?"

He leaned in and smiled, "Other jobs are involved, not just cleaning."

"I don't."

I said it sharply. I didn't look at him anymore and gripped my daughter's hand even tighter. I started walking again, angered at what he was doing, at what we both knew he had meant. It wasn't even like I'd never considered it, but I had learned to identify when someone was preying on me. Life had taught me that ability.

A bag of beans was seventy-nine cents. I bought the beans, one large onion, two roma tomatoes, two Mexican calabazas, two bags of the fideo that was three for a dollar, and the rest in green grapes for B.

We just had to make it 'til Monday.

Speck (a performance poem)

We are particles, less than rain.
The rain drizzles and runs and then evaporates and travels again,
but where do we run?
When you pull aside the thick curtain and the sunlight shoots out
and you see them by the thousands
twirling and suspended in the light
and you wonder if they were there all along
but live in a darkness or a haze that makes them invisible,
is that what we are?

Dust that settles somewhere, at the bottom of pockets or under couches
irrelevant places
waiting for just that flash of sun to be seen?

The justice I seek is immeasurable.

It's better I'm a speck, upside-down and twirling!

What could I possibly ask from the sun besides a moment of visibility
before the curtain gets shut again
because Grandma complained?

They twirl in uniform the way we all do,
seek nothing but measured movements
and the gratification of motion from the whoosh and chaotic dance
when someone makes the bed.

It's the snap of the sheet that gives us life,
that pushes us up and out but always back to the backwards dance
that leads to the wanting again.

I'm a speck despising the dust,
the dust of heat and car exhaust in your face and tired buses,
the meow of desert poverty and always the grimy film
on my black patent-leather shoes,
the walking.

Ungrateful, nasty girl who is not humble.

Not humble in her speckness!
She wants to wear the dress,
and when the sheet snaps back she pushes toward the window,
hoping for a gust of wind and a new dance
or a new settle
besides the bottom on nobody's pocket.

I don't want to kneel.

(Looks up accusingly) Born bent, if you loved me you'd let me stand!

I can't sit still in the pew,
I'm sliding and banging the soles of my shoes
against the dark smoky woodgrain,
it echoes and says:

I am here.

I want to wear the dress,
be holy and painted like Mary and the statues,
the flickering candles and plastic flowers
my aunt and I are standing at the altar
the plastic bunches
we leave are dyed blue and unnatural,
the flowers of the poor and forgotten cemeteries
you only visit once a year to water
the headstone.

Mary.

Mary. She looks at me and tells me to run.
She wants to go, too,
unfurl her hands
leave this tomb.

Mary wants something new.

The sacred is stale here and people's prayers like folded notes

and wants,
all of their lives hanging off their dusty mouths.

Mary sighs at the sight of all of them all piled up
like unopened letters
and at the faceless children,

too many to bathe and not enough water.
The wax is burning the candles into little rivers
and Mary is holding my hand,
our fingers clasped and wet.

She smells like frankincense and dried urine.

(Heaves) Somebody open the window!

Now Mary and I are running away together,
nails on her feet
the wood breaks
and our thin arms
releasing veils
raging against
the blue sky.

Guadalupe Bravo, Chih.

Nunca puedo volver al camposanto donde sepultaron a mis abuelos. Tuvieron que cerrarlo después de tanta matanza. Abaleaban a familias enteras que llegaban en luto. Cuando era niña, íbamos cada segundo de noviembre a limpiarles sus tumbas. Yo corría, recogiendo cualquier florecilla de plástico para repartirlas a las que no tenían ninguna. Recuerdo que mi padre sacaba galones de agua para limpiar los letreros. Con cuidado, emparejaban los túmulos con el azadón y dejaban dos ramos de flores de plástico, porque así mas resistirían los elementos. Después, comprábamos Cocas en vidrio y dulces de camote. Yo me quitaba las sandalias y me acostaba en la tierra como si entre las manos de Dios.

Highways

Every time I look out across that silent desert, I remember him. His face lives vivid in my mind, buried near memories that like these mountains, cannot be moved. Fifteen years have passed since I saw him last and even now as I drive, I almost expect to see him in the distance, walking slowly toward the road, dust devils erupting at his black-booted feet.

On Christmas Eve, we would take this highway to my grandparents' house in Fabens, Texas, a nearby town east of El Paso. I was the youngest of four, so it was rare I'd ever get a window seat in my father's maroon minivan, but when I would, I'd lean my forehead up against the cold glass on the way home and watch the nighttime desert silently fly by. If you looked closely, you could see hundreds of jackrabbits out, maybe even thousands, their eyes glittering across the expanse like wild diamonds. I'd lose count and would eventually give up, watching them blur against the foggy windowpane.

"Mom, cuando duermen los conejitos?"

"Las liebres son nocturnas, duermen en el día, como los búhos."

The desert was familiar to us. Fabens was surrounded by it, so when my cousins and I were bored, we'd search for 'niños de la tierra'. None of us had ever seen one, but we'd heard they were tan insects that looked like babies and even cried if you burned them with a match. We'd head about a mile out and go exploring, each one of us carrying the longest stick we could find, poking its tip into any holes we'd see.

"Watch out for rattlesnakes! If you hear a rattle, run!"

I'd look out across the sand and desert plants and wonder where all the animals were hiding. I'd think about nighttime, how things seemed freer with the absence of light.
I've always searched to find the underside of things. There was a large stone fixed into the ground in our garden, it seemed unmovable. One summer morning at dawn, I took my dad's shovel and turned it over to see what was underneath. The moment I did, hundreds of beetles and roaches scattered around my feet. I dropped the shovel and ran away in terror. My dad had to put the stone back in its place, and every time I walked by it, I knew there were things under there I never wanted to see again.

But I knew they were there.

When I got older, I never wanted to be at home. I'd drive around at night for hours, smoking joints and listening to the sound of the wind up against my car. Sometimes I'd stop at a bar, order a drink and sit there, watching. I wanted to know who would come out after sundown, as if what happened then was actual reality. If there was nowhere to go, I'd take a long road that extended all the way across the city and drive it to the end and back. I smoked a lot of weed. I was so lonely.

We perform a lot in the sunlight, don't we? The body is honest at night, we finally attend to our needs.

When I was little, I always felt like I was meant to have this huge destiny. I had visions that I would be a writer, but there was no one that saw that in me, no one to say, "This is who you are meant to become." As I grew it felt like I was getting further and further away from those dreams.

After high school, I eventually got a job as a teacher's aide in Special Education. On the weekends, I'd go to bookstores and run my hands up and down the shelves, hoping for some kind of sign. The books there seemed smug, silent. None of them would tell me how they got written. I'd go back to my car and light up.

The truth is I never intended to befriend a hitman, I'm just good at small talk.

What really happened was I was looking for a new connect. We'd been introduced by a mutual friend, and eventually he stopped taking the rolled-up twenty I'd offer and just hand me the sack, asking if I had the time to roll him a few joints instead. We'd smoke one before I'd head out.

We were driving around in my car, smoking a joint. Before that sentence, I thought what I'd heard about him was just talk.

"The walk there, I mean, at least you're still busy, you know? Holding the fucker down, sometimes even wrestling with him for a while, but the walk back, it's different. There's this silence, like, not even your mind makes a sound."

He paused, looking out of the window as we passed a tree that had been struck by lightning and survived. Half of it was a charred stump, and on its other side protruded branches, proud and brightly green-leafed.

I drove in silence, my mind a maze trying to make sense of his hands, so close to me, twisting human necks like chicken wire. I wondered if I'd gone too far in my wanting to know.

I realized my hands were shaking holding the steering wheel.

"I hate the walk after, the walk back to my car. Let me tell you, Miss Muñoz, the desert screams more at night than people do."

I thought of the desert of my childhood, of jackrabbit eyes.

He went on.

"Even the daytime. Once I was walking for what must have been hours, I'd forgotten where I parked my car. I didn't know where the fuck I was going, didn't have a compass, nothing. I'll never forget it; it was so windy that day. There were all these dust devils everywhere, they kept crossing my path, getting in my face and eyes. All of a sudden, this owl, this huge fucking brown owl just came out of nowhere. I hadn't even seen it flying around until it swooped down at me.

It got so close to me I felt its breath on my face, and then that owl looked me right in the eyes. It had its wings spread, and then it just shot up straight into the sky and disappeared. I don't know why, but at that moment I thought of my grandmother.

I'm adopted. The only thing I know about my birth mother was that she was a full blood Yaqui, a teen mom. She didn't want me, left me wrapped up in a cardboard box at a gas station. I was in the foster system for a few years until I was adopted by a white family. When I saw that owl's eyes though, they looked real familiar."

I thought of my own grandmother, then looked over at the passenger seat at him, it felt like for the first time.

"I'm native, too, Mexican and Apache. The Apache part is on my dad's side. You wanna know something? When I was little, every summer we'd take a road trip, a vacation somewhere. Most of the time my dad headed east, toward Austin or San Antonio. Anyway, off of I-10, there's a few miles where all of the mountains turn into plateaus.

I was five years old the first time I saw them. Spirits all lined up along those plateaus, watching me. Warriors. I remember not being afraid. We'd go for miles along that highway, my father driving and mother in the passenger seat, my brothers listening to music on their headphones in the middle row and I'd be in the back, staring out of the window, wondering if I was just imagining the men on the mountain. I saw them every summer.

I began to wonder if I was native. I remember asking my dad and he said no. I asked him if Indians had lived up on those flat mountains and he said no to that, too. I was a little girl, but I knew what I'd seen, it was more than imagination. I knew what ghosts were, had seen my grandpa's when he died.
When I'd see them, I would cry.

It wasn't until years later, when I was almost eighteen, that I asked my grandmother if we were native, and she told me we were Apache. Her mother Eva was full-blood, born in Bisbee, Arizona. My grandma was born in Superior, a couple of towns away.

My grandma said that Abuela Eva told a story about Geronimo, how he would visit her father when she was a little girl, and that her mother would fix him a plate. Can you believe that? Geronimo. Years later I was digging around in a used bookstore when I came across a map of Texas, of its tribes. West, Central Texas, there were Apaches there, Lipan, Mescalero. In the book, there were drawings of them, their faces painted, riding on spotted horses. I dunno. Can you believe that? It's like, how did I know?

The whole time, it had been real. To this day I'll never understand why my dad denied being native to me, if he knew all of that. My grandma said Abuela Eva left her family at fifteen, because she was being abused. She never returned."

We sat in our silence. I noticed he shook his head, then looked up to a quickly passing evangelistic billboard that read 'HELL IS REAL/Jesus Saves!'. The words were surrounded by licking yellow flames.

"I'm an evil motherfucker," he said flatly, then chuckled. "If there is a hell, I'm going to be there, getting burned up. Those little devils are probably waiting on me now, getting their marshmallows ready."

He looked over at me.

"You want to know something? When I'm with you, I feel protected, like I'm not going to die."

He cleared his throat and said, "God is near you, I can feel it. I know you're not meant to die yet, so when I'm with you I know it's not my time. I get a peace that I don't even get in my sleep. You have this future coming, I know it."

I cried silently, watching the lines on the highway disappear beyond my headlights. God. God didn't really exist to me so much. I thought of my cousins in their Sunday best, their ruffled dresses. When I was a little girl, I had recurring nightmares. I'd wake up and feel like demons were coming after me. I desperately wanted to be somewhere safe, where no evil could reach me. I'd close my eyes and imagine heaven the way a child would, with fluffy clouds and blue skies, and angels holding swords and shields, protecting me.

I wasn't that at all anymore. I didn't think any angels would come. I didn't know who or what I had become. I never mentioned that every time we were in the car together, I'd wonder if it was the last. How I'd look up at the rear-view mirror at the headlights behind us and wonder if we were being followed. Sometimes I would imagine a car suddenly pulling up and I'd see a silver barrel in my face, shots break glass, the way it would all look in slow motion. How I would see myself, body strewn and twisted on the side of the road, face smashed in like a bloody peanut, throat ragged and gasping for air.

I didn't want to die, but I was terrified of life, of everything that came with it.

"You really think I'm protecting you?"

"Yeah, I do," he said softly, as we drove into the burnt sunset that peeked over the horizon like a dozing eye.

Indian Clay

The blonde lady that visited classroom 3C that day held a wide-brimmed book that was later placed on her lap when she sat in our teacher's wooden rocking chair at the edge of the linty rug. "Please sit down Indian style," she said. We had a hard time saying her name, so she just told us to call her Mrs. K. She had come to read our class a story about an Indian girl who was learning to make clay pottery from her grandmother. Mrs. K moved her hand outward in a half-circle motion and then stopped it in midair, making the charms on her gold bracelet jangle when she said, "Many moons ago…"

I thought that sounded funny and pictured a pile of moons stacked atop one another, like the swirled blue marbles that my older brother Charlie kept hidden in his drawer next to the wallet he got for Christmas last year. Instead of paying attention, I stared at her brown sandals, how her bright red square toenails pressed downward with each movement as she rocked the chair. Mrs. K had wavy yellow hair that bloomed a pale white at the tips, like my neighbor's cocker spaniel, Romeo. I didn't like Romeo, or Mrs. K.

The Indian girl in the book lived with her tribe somewhere where there was a large field filled with sun and wild grasses, and she wore a buffalo dress her mother had made just for her. There was a part where, after sewing the dress, there was buffalo bladder left over, so her mother made her a small fringed bag from it and an even tinier, littler bag for her doll. Everyone knew she was a special girl.

I shifted and looked down at my tennies. My mom had bought them for me downtown. I remembered the day I got them, it was sunny and we woke up early to take one of the city buses from where we lived across town. The tennies were bright white and had big hot pink stars on their sides.
I had been really happy at the shoe store, so much that I even skipped out of it and made sure to hop over the little grey puddles on the sidewalk that the rain had left behind. Later that day as we waited for the bus that would take us home, the paper bottom of my snow cone collapsed and dripped blue dots all over my new shoes. My mom got upset and said I was a spoiled girl, so spoiled that I was careless with good things and that I didn't deserve anything nice.

I didn't think I was spoiled. On television, the little blonde girl in my favorite show was rich and wore a sparkly pair of fancy dress shoes that matched the big bows in her hair. In every episode, her shoes and bow were a different color. I was always growing out of shoes too fast. There were times when the only dress shoes I had were hand-me-downs from our neighbor La Señora Ruiz's granddaughter, Corina.

Corina was two years older than me and lived on the other side of town. A couple of times a year, her grandma would come by and leave me a box full of all the pretty clothes Corina had outgrown. Even used, Corina's dresses and shoes were much nicer than mine. Last summer, she owned five pairs of colored Keds, and I had found them all in the bag, unscuffed and tied together with pale twine. I was so excited; I wore them around the house even though they were still too big.

Corina would never have dripped blue snow cone on her new shoes. She was careful with her good things. My mom had said, "Es una niña fina." I didn't think I was a niña fina like Corina or the rich girl on TV, even though my mom said I was. That day I'd cried all the way home because I had disappointed her, hiding my new tennies under the seat.

I looked up and saw Mrs. K smiling at me and felt embarrassed. I didn't want her to see my feet, didn't want her to see that I had tried to rip off one of the stars but couldn't and stopped halfway, making it hang dirty and jagged on my left shoe, ugly.

In the book, the girl was saying goodbye to her family and leaving them to live with her grandmother, who wanted to teach her how to make the clay pots she was famous for, the ones with the water bird design. The first morning she was there, her grandmother woke her up extra early and took her outside to pray, and then gather clay.

At the end of the book, she was grown up and had designed extra-special clay pots for her husband-to-be's family, bright blue and flowered. Mrs. K showed us the back cover where there was an illustration of a smiling grown-up Indian woman holding a laughing brown baby in one arm, and a bright blue pot in the other.

Mrs. K said that when the girl grew up and became a grandmother, she became famous for her pottery too, just like her grandmother had been, and that she taught her own granddaughters the same.

I wondered if there was anything my mother was going to teach me that her mother had taught her.

Mrs. K asked our teacher, Mrs. Fairbanks, if it was okay to take us all outside, and then asked us to line up. We followed her silently and walked down the squeaky hall toward double doors that led out to the playground.

"There's Indian clay under everything, under all of us," she said once we were all outside. "Native-Americans used to make pottery out of it, and other things. Tools." Now she was wearing a purple shawl interwoven with green threads, and it hung carelessly off her waist, with its ends dragging on the floor. A few small shovels were passed out, but after a few minutes we were all just using our hands.

Indian clay.

"Go ahead," she said, "Gather and knead it until it's warm."

She then placed Dixie bowls filled with water on the floor and passed out small handfuls of Popsicle sticks and toothpicks. "Can you make anything? Maybe a bowl, a cup, a bird?"

I looked across the yard at my best friend Sarah, at her straight black hair and the way the strands were infused with sun. Sarah seemed shy sometimes, but she liked to laugh. I imagined Sarah and I made the best pots, so much that everyone would notice and then we'd be famous. Mrs. K left a little while after. The small bowls and plates everyone made were placed on the windowsill to dry, but by the end of the day the rounded saucers that had been carefully made got crumbly and broke. None survived. My cup, which was smooth and crisp when it was wet, was now just an ashy pile of dirt. Mrs. Fairbanks said we probably hadn't dug deep enough to where the real clay was.

Indian clay.

I looked for it somewhere else once, some summer night when I was thirteen, in our backyard underneath the honeysuckle vines. It was after the rain, and I kneeled and swatted at the ground, pulling up handfuls of sloppy-veined mud. I thought I scraped it with my fingernail.

Now I am a woman.

A woman standing in front of an oval medicine cabinet mirror. A brown face looking solemnly at itself, gums and teeth that seem terrifyingly ugly underneath the fluorescent light. "When did my pores get so big and noticeable?" I said aloud, then blinked, looking at my ruddy face. I opened the medicine cabinet mirror and took out my white clay mask. The label said the clay was collected in the rain forest and that it would help even out the crow's feet that have been forming around my eyes, and the laugh lines.

The mask made my face bone white, white-faced. There was a storm outside, and hail was hitting feverishly against the windowpane, a loud pap-pap-papping that sounded like knocking at the door, knocking that threatened to invade my attic apartment. I walked out of the bathroom into my bedroom half-expecting to find someone there, but there wasn't anyone. Sensing a sliver of movement, I asked, "Who's there?"

The rain lapped at the window and I scanned the room, all the walls, eventually settling on my collection of framed Renaissance women. Their faces all seemed different, somehow. I suspected some of them had moved from their original poses. No, I knew they had. That long-haired countess was scowling when I bought her. Now she was smiling at me, and had let her hair down, melting. I moved suddenly, hoping I'd startle her, but only the lace curtains fluttered in response.

I was suddenly aware that it was happening again, I was having another episode.

The lights flickered, everything mocking me.

Opening the medicine cabinet door, I looked until I saw a flash of metal. The manicure scissors. Sliding my thumb and index finger into the holes, I began trimming my right eyebrow, hand shaking and then not paying attention accidentally pinched a thick piece of flesh between the blades and in a whoosh pressing down hard sliced off a tilted crescent moon shape. What began as a flush pink I watched curiously become blood running fast, covering my left eye in a crimson river drip-drip-dripping on the tiled floor.

It stung. I looked into the mirror at myself. Now my eyebrow was really uneven I thought, squinted and frowned, clipping off what I felt in thickness the same amount of flesh on my other eyebrow. This time it was a bigger chunk, deep and square-shaped that caused a smarting and a line of red that quickly raced down over my other eye onto my cheek and chin, staining my silk robe and spreading like black ink dyeing.

Dyeing. I looked up and smiled into the mirror. Pincushion, pincushion, where was the Indian clay?

Mercy

We seek mercy and not
grace.

Grace,
we don't know it.

Tell me,
hold it in your palm
rub its mouth-
truth.

Mercy,
being held down
but held.
Mercy
mercy but not grace
your mouth won't give
it,
and always my eyes that perceive too well
the spirits in the room
that gather and collapse
seeking mercy
mercy but not
grace.

Spirits

The spirits are always here. They always have and will, lining the dusty streets, walking toward eternity or nowhere in particular. Most belief systems and people want to believe that souls slip out of bodies and then leave this realm in one way or another, but not all of them leave. Some just stay, wearing that flowered dress or brown loafers they always did, walking the streets and neighborhoods downtown, taking the bus and back again.

When we met, he told me that he didn't believe in God, or in spirits. He said he couldn't believe in anything he couldn't see.

I don't know why I stayed, but I did and eventually, even stopped mentioning the spirits. I didn't tell him I had a feeling that most of the spirits who stay behind stay because they couldn't imagine past the physical world.

Months after I left, I realized he hadn't seen me, either. The shadow parts, the hidden wonders I kept. He saw only what he could see, and that kind of sight had made me dull. He wanted me to trade my eyes for his, so he'd be less afraid.

All the world's magic and miracles live halfway in the spirit world! This is who I am. I've learned to grind the root to find medicine, and I have found answers in the visions that come from sleeping by ceremonial fires.

I don't want anyone's eyes but my own.

Cafecito

"That's what happens a lot, eh. Medicine women used to be older, you know, the grandmother who collected wisdom slowly, after passing through the stages of life until they're an elder. That's how it was, young women were too busy having babies and then raising them, so the medicine usually found them a little later. We're living in different times now.

Maybe it's because people are getting sicker and sicker, but medicine women are waking up earlier, many of them hear the call in their teens or twenties, and they still have to date, you know? They still have to grow up and pass the stages of life, but they're conscious to their path. I heard someone say once that medicine women meet the sickest men, the ones who need the most medicine. Ain't that a motherfucker."

"Yeah, it is," I laughed. "Damn. Well what are we supposed to do? I had been single for years, you know? Being a single mom and writing my stories, and yeah, I was depressed. Writers are depressed. You've got all this passion inside you that culminates and inevitably requires release, literarily, sexual, but there are no damn warriors anywhere. You either go the celibate route and eventually lose it, or you give in to the desire and share energy with someone who doesn't understand you. I hate it. I hate the cycle. We give, they take."

"You don't control anyone's enlightenment."

"I know I don't. It's not who I am." I stared into my coffee. "It's not. I'm just tired, you know, tired of love being some dried-up river everyone is squeezing drops out of. I feel like I can't communicate freely. Love stops and starts, like traffic. Sometimes you get on a smooth highway and really fly, and then that highway turns into a two-lane country road. That's what happened, when it turned into the road, he got out of the car. Where's the partner that, when there's mud, gets out and helps push the damn thing?"

"Why are you in a car?" she asked.

"What?"

"Yeah. Why are you even in a car, you know? Highways, country roads, traffic
lights, in the world of the car there exists the plane, somewhere above us all. Somewhere above us there's a chingona flying her own plane with her daughter strapped in, both of them wearing some hot-pink aviator goggles."

Tears pooled and then ran down my face. "Yeah." I laughed. "I want to be that
chingona."

La Chingona

But I don't want to chingarte. Through generations of relationship archetypes appearing and reappearing in our personal lives and ancestral histories, I feel like we've seen enough to know what abuse is, how it permeates and is cyclical.

There's violence in the word. In Spanish, chingar means to fuck, or be fucked. Maybe even to rape. Mexicanos have been called, "Hijos de la Chingada." Rape insists on control, on power. To chingarte would be to humiliate you, and I don't want to do that.

I am a chingona that doesn't want to chingar anyone. I want to nurture, be nurtured. I want you to lift your chin.

One of my greatest fears is having been born with bad instincts. I've made so many decisions I've later regretted. In the wild, if you're a jaguar that can't hunt, or run, you eventually die. As a deer, if you can't outrun the jaguar, igual. I'm a woman who is sometimes not so sure I will survive. I've always had a sort of frailty about me, a vulnerability, like maybe I can't hunt, or maybe I won't outrun the jaguar.

As a child, I would regularly get my feelings hurt and sob onto my mother's shoulder. The trauma would seep out of me, it always has.

Scars

The grandmothers say that when a cut isn't healed right, it becomes infected, and even if there's later a scar, the skin that lines it will always be frail.

> "Mejor abrir la cortada otra vez y limpiarla bien, darle poquito aire para que esta vez si se cierre y se sane."

That's where it begins, the ceremonial path, when you see your heart, body and mind's scars and decide that you're brave enough to look at them, maybe pry them open again and clean them with mint and lavender, so you heal correctly. Some of those scars happened when you were a baby.

Some while you were in your mother's womb and some of them, even before that.

Rocio Cihuacoatl

"Dime, a que le temes tanto?" the abuela asked,
her dark pupils focused on the parts of myself I could not
bear to witness

"Es que, tengo miedo de que me voy a morir," I choked out,
sobbing

"No me quiero morir."

"Muchacha, todos nos morimos, pero entiende, no es tu tiempo, si te ibas a morir ya te hubieras muerto,
tantos cuartos oscuros donde te metiste.
Mentiras, no temes la muerte!

Temes vivir."

Altar is me

Coatlicue doesn't speak,
she watches you with silent eyes that follow into every room
and out
the rock figure by the altar where you sometimes forget and
leave your keys
coerced into silence
she sees
vases of water and white flowers embroidered tablecloths the
flame floating on the wick isn't enough
hair neatly braided the Coatlicue in you
doesn't speak.

Recently I nearly died
it wasn't Jesus who saved me
Jesus, I have tried to speak to since I was a child
walked into churches and kneeled talked to his mother surrounded by roses I have begged all my life for a sign
for a moment of miracle
asked for mercy humbly on wooden benches
wearing white Mexican dresses
recently I nearly died.

Altar is me
the cosmos
copal trickling down the coal thick smoke and
Coyolxauqui's broken body

I: universe
starry limbed: broken and suspended in stone but surrounded
by galaxies
the flint, the rock, the spark
pools of water
altar is me.

Latas

Tu sexo no te salvará

Cómo no lo sabes ya
después de tantos cuerpos que como latas has abierto
y
sin embargo
sigues
hambriento

Dorada

Polvoréame dorada
con tus manos de ateísta
y con tu boca moteada de tinta
declara que no soy sagrada
y
lánzame fuera de tu ventana,
figurilla rara.

No me molesta ser chiquita.
Mas prefiero ser la
basurilla animada por el viento
que
estatua bronceada sentada en la plaza,
monumento olvidado a caricias y poesías
pasadas.

Fui. tu. nopal.

Te dije una vez
que tomo poca agua
que tomo poca agua
te dije una vez.

Me contestaste-
más de eso,
me juraste
que amabas a mi tierra asoleada
y te acostaste
a mis pies.

Ahora me dices
que amas
las raíces mojadas
de una flor llamada
clavel.

Si las flores
prefieres,
nomás recuerda que
son pronto a la
muerte.

Año por año
yo las he visto nacer, crecer y

con el frio,
caer.

Pero esta guerrera de espinas,
ni el fuego la mueve.
Fuego quemando mi frente,
nopalito fuerte.

Nunca podría ser flor
nomás para
tenerte.
Vete.
Déjame sola
con mi desierto
y no regreses.

Tú y yo sabemos
que ni raíces
tienes.

Potranca Blanca

Ya no me reconocerías,
querido.

Mis ojitos árabes
que amabas tanto
con tiempo han cambiado
y he madurado.

Tú,
que primero quebraste candados
en mi mente y en mi cuerpo dañado,
tú, alas de ave; que raro
que ahora me encuentre encadenada
a la guía de tus manos.

No te olvido,
solo guardo.

Solo guardo.

Con tus brazos tiernos
me montabas
y
calmamente me llevabas
caminando por tu rancho
en tu silencio

me enseñaste
tu tierra sagrada,
las cruces
enterradas
en tu cuerpo,

en tu cama.

Tu piel
la recorría como camino
abierto,
tu espalda dulce carretera,
me llevaba a
pueblos nuevos.

"No me ames," me decías.
"No me ames, Palomita."

Y yo, potranca blanca
recorría,
carreteras por tu cuerpo
sino por solo
otro día.

El Rey de las Milpas

Pasan trenes, trenes pasan.
Pero/ los trenes/ no/
tienen casa.
Buscan
y/ buscan/
y al final/
nada.
Los trenes no saben nada.

Él.
Él camina.

Cuando no camina,
maneja.
Parece que tiene mapas escondidos
en sus venas,
él,
que dejo
su pueblo detrás
en búsqueda de
nuevas cosechas,
él.

Me dice que quiere volver al
campo,
quiere ver a sus

hermanos.

Me enseña fotos,
fotos plegadas en sus manos
y le beso los labios
tristes,
le pido que me platique,
como pasó,
que el Rey de las Milpas
existe aquí
rodeado por cemento
y
ciudades tan sombrosas
y grises.

Solo me mira y sonríe.

El Rey de las Milpas,
no creo que lo conocerías.

Hay un hombre sagrado
acostado en un cuarto
en una ciudad muy
torcida.

Me hace el amor y después,
me platica
como arriesgo
su vida

y se colgó de La Bestia para
cruzar la frontera
y eludir a
la migra.

Lucecitas para Ayotzinapa

Ahora que/ vamos a hacer/ buscando cuarenta y tres luciérnagas/
con/
frascos de miel/
ahora que/ vamos a hacer/

Dice la alquimia que las esencias se transmutan
solo con intención-
leña a polvo,
polvo a leña,
los ciclos acaban
como se empiezan
y no hay materia
que se transforma
a nada.

Históricamente,
el silencio del fuego nunca ha servido
para
ocultar los gritos de las bocas
cerradas
y la gasolina no fue hecha
para derramar en las caras,
en una estaca de cuerpos.

Hay una madre en su cama llorando
como niña en su infancia,

exigiendo justicia como alimento
pero
no le dan nada.

Una mañana guardando el silencio,
ella carga su arma.

Cuidado con la que ha perdido todo-
ya no le pueden quitar nada.

México, cuarenta y tres luciérnagas calcinadas
han encendido las puertas de tu casa,
dieron luz a tu palacio empolvado-
un manojo de gusanos
retorciéndose por plata.

A Cuauhtémoc le quemaron los pies los europeos
pero el Tata nunca se dio.
Sus huesitos derritiendo
candentes de valor.

Los guerreros nunca mueren,
solo se transmutan,
cambian de color.

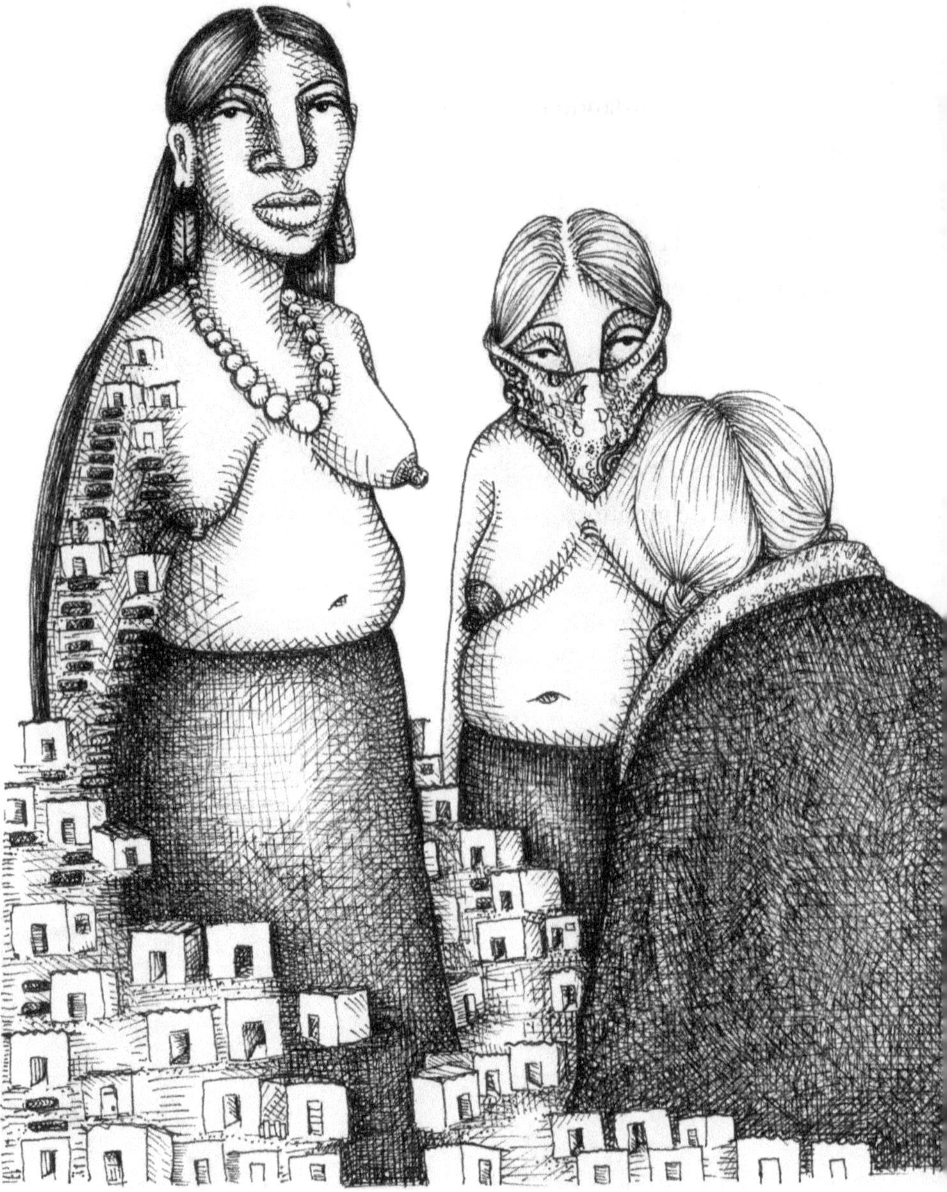

Las Diosas

Las Diosas viven en casas de cartón;
papeles desechados.
Toman el agua que vive en los
charcos,
caminan solas por calles oscuras sin nombre
marcado.

Las Diosas celebran
debajo de las revoluciones.

De periódicos cosen vestidos
y hacen fiestas en los callejones,
construyen moños de todos los colores
usando bolsas de plástico
y cordones.

Cuidan de las niñas que viven sin
dulces realidades,
vendiendo gomas de chicle en galaxias siderales
en puentes de plomo que separan dos lenguajes
y unen los vicios
comunales.

Cuidan de las mujeres
vendiendo su piel en las calles,
cuerpos sagrados

usando disfraces.

Corren detrás de carros gritando,
pero como todo lo hacen cantando,
no las escucha
nadie.

Las Diosas no duermen.

Esperan afuera de salones de baile por jovencitas
que están encomendadas a ellas
por humildes
madrecitas.

Las Diosas viven en casas de cartón;
cajas de refri con palabras escurridas
son sencillas-
no existen sentadas en sillas divinas,
o altares con fruta y cosecha de milpas.

Dicen, "Dáselo a las vivas

lovelettertoMichoacán

Where do you keep your gun
never says he loves me
but he loves the
revolution,
my body brown and crossed.

Urgent hours
unfolding maps and timing planes,
the roses in the blue glass vase sit
coral and tilted.

Held up by the prayers of your mother
and all of the women who know your anxious face lit up
in fleeting moments crowded airports bus stops
their shawls draped around shoulders bent on tiptoes for a last touch
of your militant mouth.

I waited then as I do now.

Awake
a warrior waits for the right conditions
my silence a siren blaring,
switching,
we are living
on borrowed

time and marrow.

He's packing duffel bags with equipment
and ammunition
I'm pacing
don't know what language
would reach him-

Te vas a donde los cuerpos
cuelgan de los
arboles sagrados-

Michoacán,
por las noches me duelen los huesos,
despierto de espanto.

Navaja de muelles,
solo tú me sacas lo malo
mi amor
respaldado

Soldada;
el que te caza
lo incendio,
lo mato.

Michoacán,
solo tu entiendes
mi amor ominoso,

my ominous love.

Iztaccíhuatl,
volcanic

Fluorescent grey ash
I
swallow things up
and turn them
to stone,
whole cities, bridges
and roads.

Michoacán,
I erupt all alone
when you pack up
and go.

Uninhabitable

Like the land, white men have found me uninhabitable,
impossible to navigate, arid

Even in my love, violently benevolent
like flash floods in July
pulling up concrete

Whisper to me lover, sultrily, how deep down you think I'm a beast
descendant of muscular beasts
working the land beasts
leathered by the sun bruised blue-black beasts
my blood's origin some dusty place where poverty eats its children
curled and gasping

Dilated pupil contracting;
cornered I will lunge,
will never give
will never allow you the illusion of my godlessness

The prism of my cunt: God's eye
glint that when angled with the sun
sees all

Desert Utero

And you've watched this whole time
occasional intermediary
observed the thick dust covering us
where we're forced to lower our eyes
to keep walking in line
opaqued by unrelenting desert winds

The sand paints the sky bland
in this place where
young women are engulfed
placed in their graves at birth
consecrated by the crosses piercing their wombs

Sadist
how you take from some
to give to others

My mother's placenta
stretched to nourish too many bellies, my father's and brothers'
and mine, and the
corporate beast that took the rest of
her body
now frail
cancer
the factory

I regret ever taking
a mouthful of her sangre
even in utero when I was choiceless
her arms outstretched

"Mamá, no te mueras," I whisper, angry at Dios for all the mothers he takes
to feed the corporate beasts that claim him

God and I know that somewhere a white woman thrives because
of what her father stole from us,
my mother's placenta a thin red line extending to her mouth, too

I can't pray to you while
she smiles and bellows, "Thank you, Jesus,"
her belly filled with our blood

Sempervivum

I sat down carefully alongside the edge of the bed, our old bed that was now hers alone. I'd left weeks ago, hastily packed all my clothing on a night she was working her shift at the clinic. At the time I'd felt relief at the sight of my bags by the door, and since I'd been gone I hadn't felt a moment of regret, until now.

"I shouldn't have come," I said flatly.

"Don't say that, please, I was hoping you'd return."

The truth was that I didn't want to be there because I'd already moved on. It made it difficult to focus on her, and I felt shame for it. Sensing her discomfort, I averted my eyes downward and focused on the blanket, at its yellow bird pattern. I reached down and traced its aquamarine stitching with my forefinger. The birds were sewn diagonally and seeing them reminded me of the day we'd purchased the blanket. She had bought it because I'd said I imagined that the birds were all flying toward a sun they could not see.

I'd loved her then and had really believed if I could stay with anyone, it was her. I scanned the room quickly, wanting to remember as much as I could before leaving.

"Isi, I have to go now." I mouthed the words softly.

"Please don't leave again. I've missed you so much, everything here reminds me of you, of us. You are the first woman I've been with, this whole time, there's only been you. I can't imagine moving on, us living separate lives. Haven't you missed me?"

"I have missed you. It's just that I don't know how to stay, anywhere, with anyone. I thought I always made that clear. I tried to be honest from the beginning."

From my peripheral I saw her face crumble, her eyes looking upward and welling up.

"I've been checking your log-ins. I noticed you haven't filed for a clinic transfer. I knew you moved out but were still somewhere in the city. Is it a new woman?"

"You entered my log-in history? I didn't even consider you would do that, that's so not like you." I rubbed my eyes. "Look it doesn't even matter, Isi, we both know we hadn't been happy for months."

It was painful to speak to her so harshly. I wasn't even sure why I'd returned. It hurt me inside to be here and be reminded so clearly how we'd met and now, what we'd become. Isi embodied the home I'd always imagined. I once heard someone say that you shouldn't make homes out of people, but sometimes you can't help it. They themselves let you in, give you the key, let you lay and heal in the soft blanket they keep inside.

That's how it had felt with Isi, an instant attraction. Everything about her seemed familiar.

I'd just checked into a new global clinic and was standing in line for dinner. She was a busy nurse on a break. We'd chatted some in line and decided to sit together while we ate.

"So, you're Grey. We received a briefing on you, on your condition. I couldn't believe I'd finally get to meet one."

"One what?" I'd asked slyly and smiled.

"Um, you're a modified, right? We treated one here years ago, a man, but that was before I was assigned here. I've always wondered, what's it like? I always thought modifieds were a myth. I didn't even believe you all really existed until I went to nursing school. There's so few of you left in the world. The last I heard there were twelve."

"Ah well, yes, we, I mean, I exist," I laughed, feeling my face flush. "I survived the modification at age seven and I guess you could say I'm one of the lucky ones, though to be honest, I don't feel lucky. But I rarely get sick or have any ill effects. Overall, I'm healthy. Because I need so little water to survive, I tend to get low on my water levels. I'll sometimes forget to drink water for months and then start feeling sick."

"Please excuse my intrusive questions, but do you date?" She looked embarrassed. "You don't have to answer that," she said. "It's just, you're very beautiful."

I blushed. "Thank you. I do date, actually."

"I can't imagine any men would mind your condition. Again, I'm sorry for my stupid questions. I just never thought I'd meet a real modified."

> "It's okay. You can ask anything you want. I don't mind answering your questions. They're not stupid. As for men, I like them sometimes, though I mostly date women. I don't think any of my lovers have cared much about my condition. At least not at first."

> "Oh, I, I'm sorry, I'd just assumed. I've always thought about it, you know, dating women. I spend a lot of time here in the clinic. There aren't any women here to even consider. I have never uh, been with a woman."

We both laughed nervously. In that silence our eyes met, pupils large.

I've spent my life traveling between global clinics, waiting in airports, searching the faces of strangers as they walked by. From the outside, everyone seems somewhat similar. We share the same basic body parts and sizes, but nobody really knows what anyone holds inside. You can sit right next to someone, touch their body and even enter it and still not really know.

Like myself, for instance, I'm not fully human. I am a surviving 'modified', one of very few left in the world.

Our relationship grew from that first meeting. She'd never been with another woman and I was afraid of getting hurt, or of hurting her. Still, I fell in love with Isi, more than I ever had with anyone. Loving a nurse felt natural to me. Throughout the years, so many other partners had seemed fascinated by my medical condition until ultimately, it became a source of confusion, even pity. Isi was curious about my modification but not at all afraid.

We'd spent almost four years together.

"Isi, you know I've never stayed anywhere, with anyone. I don't know another form of living except constant change. Nothing has ever been steady and that is what brings me comfort. I'm sorry. This really isn't about another woman. I'm planning to file a transfer in a few months, there's a spot opening at the Mexico City clinic. I feel drawn there, like I should go for reasons I still don't fully understand."

I was four years old when the recalls began. Due to industrial contamination, the water supply on Earth had gotten so dangerously low that a global water conservation law was passed. I, along with four hundred low-income children, was forcibly dosed with an experimental vaccine, a coagulant that converted all the liquid in my body into a gel-like substance. The vaccine was created using cell cultures from a certain type of succulent, and with it, scientists believed that the human body could be modified to need less water to survive.

According to the media at that time, legislation was passed so quickly that there wasn't even time to protest. There were no advocates for us. Our parents were told we would be pioneers, the first of our kind. If they complied, they'd be given $50,000 and we'd have free healthcare for the rest of our lives. The whole family, even my brothers.
We were all tested, but they only wanted me.

My parents were assured the vaccine was safe and that it had already been tested in other parts of the world and that all those subjects survived, thrived, even. They were told the vaccine would make us even healthier than before. The modification was permanent, and with it from then on my body would only need about a cup of water a month to operate.

My parents tried their hardest to get me excited about being modified. I don't remember feeling anything at all.

It wasn't until I was an adult that I found out that my inoculation was carried out by one of the inventors of the vaccine himself, a brilliant hematologist named Dr. Tabrizi. Most of what I remember about him is his smiling face and how pleased he was that my blood type was O positive.

"Do you know what a cactus is?" he asked, taking my temperature.

"A cactus is a plant that collects up all the water around it and keeps it inside. Some are also classified as succulents. There is a succulent called Sempervivum. It looks kind of like a flower. When I was a little boy growing up in Iran, my mother had them growing all around our house, in pots, coffee cans. The name means, 'live forever'.

These little green rosettes survive and flourish even with no water. This plant can grow all over the world, it is universal and much smarter than humans, and you, you are a very brave and a very special little girl. When you wake up from a long nap, just like the Sempervivum, you will get through any condition just fine."

I watched him prepare a large needle and winced when he stuck it into my neck.

"Mom, me duele!"

My mother was then instructed to keep me in bed for one month.

In my deep sleep, I had dreams of floating in water, alone and suspended, and then suddenly feeling like I was being pulled through dark whirlpools. There was a pair of arms that would find me in the water, its hands on my shoulders pushing and holding me down. I've met other modifieds and every one of them has described the same pulling, the same arms.

I awoke one morning thirty-three days later. I felt very hungry. The next day, I asked my mother if I could go outside and play with my best friend Louie. Her face darkened. She told me that Louie had not survived the injection. I think that was the first moment I knew something in me had changed. I wanted to cry but couldn't, not like before. My tears were gone.

There was a solemnness living deep in the center of me, a feeling I'd never felt before. I walked outside, startled by the bright sun on my face. The world around me seemed strange. I didn't understand why I had survived, and Louie hadn't. I wondered about the arms, if they had drowned him. For the first time, I felt I understood death.

Louie wasn't the only casualty from the inoculations. Two hundred children never woke up, and the rest of us became very afraid, wondering if we were next. Even though so many died from the extreme physical conditions the vaccine caused, just as Dr. Tabrizi predicted, I survived.

The water shortage had been a fluke. The earth's water supply stabilized within five years and especially after so many deaths, the project was abandoned, and its details classified. For years, there was talk of a reversal medication being developed. I was expectant and put my name on several waiting lists for studies, but none of them ever came into fruition. The surviving modifieds and I were tested every three months for any changes in our internal organs and limbic systems.

At fifteen, I moved to New York City to live at the first global clinic that the United Nations fought to have opened for any surviving modifieds. I was given a lifetime pension and unlimited medical care, though I very rarely got sick.

By then, I knew I was attracted to women, and traveling allowed me to fully exist in the way I knew I couldn't have back home.

I never wanted to see my childhood town ever again. More clinics were founded, although more and more of us kept dying. Remaining modifieds became a fascinating medical anomaly.

For years I made my home in many women, all galaxies I enjoyed exploring. Isi was the one I'd loved most. A part of me wanted to stay with her, but when I was informed there were plans to open a small global clinic in Mexico City, I knew I had to go. Something was pushing me there.

"I'm so sorry, Isi," I uttered, then stood up and walked toward the door and looked back for a moment before walking out, shutting it behind me.

In the stillness that remained, I heard the measure of my own breathing, of my own heart that through it all still pulsed and fought.

Gris Muñoz is a frontera poet, performer and essayist. Her work has been published in *The Rumpus*, *Bitch Media*, *Queen Mob's Teahouse* and will be featured in the upcoming Cutthroat Press *Chicanx* Anthology. She is currently commissioned to write the biography of acclaimed L.A. artist, Fabian Debora. Gris is Chicana of Apache descent.

Los Dos is the husband and wife duo of frontera graphic artists Ramon and Christian Cardenas. Ramon is a Filipino-American visual artist and co-founder of Maintain, a multimedia artist network formed in part to curate cultural events in the El Paso/Juárez region. Christian is a mixed media artist from Cd. Juárez, Chih. México. Her portfolio includes a series of lithographs, screenprints and illustrations addressing the ongoing femicides in her native city. The artists create public art installations as well as gallery work to form a dialogue between the cities and their people. They have exhibited their work in El Paso, Austin, San Antonio, San Francisco, Ciudad Juárez, Chihuahua City, Puebla City, Oaxaca City, and CDMX. Their work has been featured by *Remezcla*, *PBS*, *Vice*, and *The Washington Post*. @losdos_maintainstudio

CPSIA information can be obtained
at www.ICGtesting.com
Printed in the USA
BVHW031815310821
615695BV00003B/779